Pursuing Your Purpose With Passion

By

Regina Mixon

Pursuing Your Purpose With Passion

ISBN: 978-0-9820699-1-2
Published by
REGS Books, LLC
P O Box 5397
Torrance, CA 90510
www.regsbooks.org
email: regsbooks@yahoo.com

All scripture quotations (unless noted otherwise) are taken
from The Holy Bible, King James Version
Copyright © 1994 by The Zondervan Corporation

All rights reserved. No part of this book may be reproduced in
any form without the written permission of the author, except
in the case of brief quotations embodied in church-related
publications, critical articles or reviews.

Printed in the United States of America. All rights reserved
under International Copyright Law. Contents and/or cover
may not be reproduced in whole or in part in any form without
the express written consent of the author.

SPECIAL DEDICATION

This manuscript is dedicated to the memory
of a dear sister,

Rosemary Couch

Who made her transition on
Sunday, April 27, 2008.
Although you are not physically here with us,
the memories of you still exist and
Your spirit lives on in *Sisters of the Word!*

ACKNOWLEDGMENTS

In pursuit of this writing I have had many who encouraged, inspired, taught, pushed and motivated me. So, to Pastor W. Terrell Snead, II, Gail Marie Hughes-King, Jane Cazabat, Linda Kinchelow, Felonesecia West, Jewel Diamond Taylor (Women on the Grow), Annette Jones Davidson, Della Mixon, Dorothy Mozeke, Joy Ferlauto (TBN), Jackie Graham Chapman, Cynthia Lewis Combs, Rose Thornton Kinsey, Joy Lewis (The 411), Deborah Granger (Quiet Time Radio and Publishing), Deborah Banks, The Bio Shoppe, Raena Banks Neal, Terry McNulty, Thea (Black Christian Book Distributors), Lori Carter (Smiley Books), Sheila James (Christian African American Booksellers Association), Pastor Ron Hill of Love & Unity COGIC, Dr. Netreia Carroll, Marsha Sumner (Heaven1580AM), Shyeta Mozeke, Victoria Gipson, Shiemetre Brown-Smith, Paul (Kings Highway Web Design), Dr. Carroll (Affordable Publishing), Keisha Fuller Thomas and Emily Nicole Mixon…I say "thank you". Your support, critique, advice and assistance in whatever way helped to make yet another dream come true. For this, I give my heartfelt thanks.

INTRODUCTION

In 2006, at our Women of Purpose and Determination Anniversary, God gave me this message to deliver to the group present. Pleasantly surprised by the positive responses I received from the hearers; as a result, I was led to put the principles in a book format -**PURSUING YOUR PURPOSE WITH PASSION.**

This book is filled with practical steps that will help the reader pursue his/her purpose in life with such passion that no one can stop one from reaching their goal.

I encourage you to keep this book with you and refer to it from time to time, especially when things don't quite manifest as you desire. Prayerfully, it will inspire you continue to press in spite of the obstacles in your path.

So read the "PPP's", as many people affectionately refer to them, and walk in the newness of life. Renew your commitment to yourself and to God and begin to pursue your purpose with passion like never before.

Table of Contents

Special Dedication — iv
Acknowledgments — v
Introduction — vi

Step One — Pray
Step Two — Prepare
Step Three — Plan/Prioritize
Step Four — Partnerships
Step Five — Persist
Step Six — Promote
Step Seven — Patience
Step Eight — Promises

Conclusion
Suggested Readings

Pray

"Therefore I say unto you, What things soever ye desire, when ye pray, believe that ye receive them, and ye shall have them."
Mark 11:24

"Pray without ceasing."
I Thess. 5:17

"Evening, and morning, and at noon, will I pray, and cry aloud: and he shall hear my voice."
Psalm 55:17

STEP ONE
Pray

Jewel Diamond Taylor often reminds us to "keep the main thing the main thing". What is the main thing required in pursuit of anything? The answer to that question is simple - prayer. First and foremost, ask God to reveal what His purpose is for your life. Ask Him for guidance, wisdom, knowledge and understanding. Prayer opens the door for God to do just that.

Matthew 6:33 tells us to seek first the kingdom of God and His righteousness. Prayer is one way of doing this. It is keeping "the main thing the main thing" or, in other words, first things first.

We often have an idea as to what we should be doing. By praying **every step** of the way we will know that we are exactly where we need to be at the exact time we need to be there. Prayer assures us that we are walking in the will of God and pursuing all that he desires us to accomplish.

Sometimes we think that we can handle situations on our own or maybe that we know what we want or should be doing at any given time. I encourage you to not make that mistake. The way to KNOW that you are doing what you need to do is by being in constant communication with God.

Prayer is not one sided. It is a two way conversation between you and God. When you pray, take the time to listen to what the Spirit is saying to you. God speaks to each of us. We have to be receptive. Invite the Holy Spirit into your life and be willing to listen and follow the instructions He gives you.

The Bible tells us that we should pray without ceasing. So, whether you are a believer or a non-believer, try prayer. In doing so, you will "keep the main thing the main thing" and allow God to minister to your spirit.

Never minimize the power of prayer. As the saying goes, "much prayer, much power; little prayer, little power; no prayer, no power". There is power in praying. Tap into it and in doing so you are obeying the scriptures and assuring the fulfillment of your purpose.

Prepare

"Make adequate preparation before elevation."
Jewel Diamond Taylor

"For which of you, intending to build a tower, sitteth not down first, and counteth the cost, whether he have sufficient to finish it."
Luke 14:28-30

"Prepare thy work without, and make it fit for thyself in the field: and afterwards build thine house."
Proverbs 24:27

STEP TWO
Prepare

Proper preparation is vital to the success in pursuit of anything. Prepare by developing a lifestyle of learning. Prepare by educating yourself on the topics or subject matter you are pursuing. Prepare by networking with those who are doing what you aspire to do. Proper preparation is a key ingredient to the success of anything.

In preparing, don't be afraid of making mistakes. Remember it is a learning process. Your purpose is a journey and not a destination. Learn anything and everything about the things you are pursuing. Mistakes happen along the way…it's a process.

I stress education much as many times we don't realize the importance of continual education. As a teenager I neglected classes in geography, history, and didn't care much for English. I thought, "Why do I need to know this?" What relevance does it have as far as what I want to do in life? Years ago I began to fully understand why these were important.

How does one know what country they want to go to should the desire to travel abroad become a pursuit of theirs? What about an author or a speaker? How can one effectively communicate orally or in writing without having the basic knowledge of good communication skills?

English. Who cares about nouns, pronouns, adjectives, adverbs, conjunctions and all of that stuff? Why is it so important to know these things? How can one even have a decent conversation with someone without knowing this? How can a writer put two sentences together that makes any sense to the reader without having a basic knowledge of English? Impossible!

One desire of mine is to travel abroad. In order to do that, I need to know the customs of the people there so as not offend the natives. I need to know whether it is a continent or a country. I need to know what the dress and weather conditions are at the location I plan to attend. I need to know where it is in relation to where I am.

Had I been more focused in some of the classes I neglected I would not have to do such extensive research now in finding these things out. But, it's not too late.

What relevance does studying history have in pursuing a purpose? You may be considering finding out why certain things are now taking place. Studying history provides this and other valuable information.

Please allow me to include that in school I was an honor student and actually loved school. Oftentimes I have wondered what or where would I have been by now had I focused more on some subjects neglected. You've often heard the saying, "If I knew then what I know now"…Again, it's not too late.

Another wonderful way of preparing for pursuit of your purpose is by listening to the advice and wisdom of older people in your lives. This is still a part of learning. You would be amazed at some of the things these people can share with you.

In listening to some of the older family members in my own family, I learned so much as to why certain things happened as well as what shaped and molded their way of thinking. I was absolutely shocked to hear stories of past events relayed to me through them.

Believe this or not, but even our young can assist us in pursuit or preparation for pursuing our purpose. Wisdom can come from any source that God chooses to use. Don't be so quick to talk so much to show how smart you are; be willing to listen. And when doing so, analyze the information you've received. It just may be something that will help you go to the next level in pursuit of your goals, visions or dreams.

Be as Abraham Lincoln said in pursuit of your purpose…study and prepare yourself and some day your chance will come. Jewel Diamond Taylor also has a tape entitled "Preparation before Elevation" which is an excellent resource. Preparation is the second most important key in pursuit of your purpose.

And for those that don't know, Abraham Lincoln found his way into the White House. And Jewel Diamond Taylor is an award winning, world renowned speaker, teacher, radio/TV personality. Preparation always comes before elevation.

In preparing, you should be the biggest investor in you, investing your time in education; your talents and your money in preparation.

Reading is FUNDAMENTAL! Read the newspapers. Read books. READ!

If you're not preparing now it is not too late to start. Today should work well for you. Get prepared. Don't wait to do it; do it now.

Plan

If one fails to plan, they plan to fail.
Plan to win!

Prioritize

Work on your most important tasks
FIRST!
To do, to do, to do!

STEP THREE
Plan/Prioritize

Habakkuk 2:2-3 states that we should "write the visions on the table and make it *plain* so that those who read it may run with it". It goes on to say that "though it tarries, wait for it because at the set time, the appointed time it will speak". What does that verse mean in simple terms? It means that in order to pursue your purpose you have to plan and prioritize.

Writing the vision down is the very first step to planning. Without a written plan one has no clear direction for where his life is going. He is just living haphazardly. In other words, life is taking him on a rollercoaster. Not having a plan allows others to basically control our time, talents and money. We give power to everyone else to determine who we are and where we're going. Take back your power!

Write out your personal mission statement. In Steven Covey's book, "The Seven Habits of Highly Effective People", he suggests starting with the end in mind.

He encourages people to write out their obituary and include in it what you WANT people to say about you when you die and work from that. Begin with the end in mind.

If your purpose in life is to minister to others through song, pray, prepare and write down everything you need to do to accomplish that goal. Take voice lessons or join a choir. Believe in yourself and know that if you take continual steps, God will put you at the right place at the right time with the right people to make it happen.

In the Bible one scripture that I absolutely love found in Isaiah 43:18 tells us to forget everything that has happened because God is doing a new thing. Writing the vision on the table and creating an action plan are vital steps to take towards the new thing.

When you're planning and prioritizing do it for YOUR life only. Don't be a busybody, as I have been, trying to plan everyone else's life. Your mission statement, your goals, visions and dreams and your plans are what should be included in YOUR pursuit of your purpose.

Write down your values without compromising. It costs us too much and adds a lot of unnecessary pain and sorrow.

Develop a strategic plan with corresponding action steps. What do I mean by this? First of all decide what you are going to do and then break each thing down into bite-sized pieces. Looking at the big picture can be overwhelming. Breaking it down into small steps enables you to develop an action plan to accomplish your goal.

Set target dates. Even if you miss the date, don't stop moving forward. Set a new date and keep taking steps.

Prioritize your actions. I suggest doing no more than seven at a time; some may want to start with three. Even if you start with one, get started.

Once you've accomplished those, move on to the next set of items. Don't overwhelm yourself. Remember, it's a journey.

Allow me to remind you that *life* happens. Even with the best laid plans things happen to temporarily distract us on our journey.

Sickness, deaths, financial challenges – these things can and will happen. Don't get discouraged when things don't go exactly as planned. Simply regroup and start again where you are.

I have to confess that I am a controller in recovery. That phrase was used by one of my sisters at church, and it fit my personality to a "T". When things would not go exactly as I had planned I would have a fit. I have a habit of keeping post-it notes or some type of list of things to do items at all times. If I accomplished everything on the list, I would be on cloud nine. If I didn't, I would go into a tizzy. Remember, I'm in recovery. Don't stress out if things don't go your way. Life happens.

Plan and prioritize. Take the time to celebrate your accomplishments, big or small. By the inch it's a cinch but by the yard it does tend to get a bit hard. Inch your way to your purpose!

Partnerships

"Two are better than one; because they have a good reward for their labor"
Ecclesiastes 4:9

"For I say, through the grace given unto me, to every man that is among you, not to think of himself more highly than he ought to think: but to think soberly, according as God hath dealt to every man the measure of faith. For as we have many members in one body, and all members have not the same office: so we, being many, are one body in Christ, and every member one of another."
Romans 12:3-5

Without a team, a dream is just a dream.

STEP FOUR
Partnerships

Establish partnerships with people who can help you as you pursue your purpose. These individuals may or may not share your vision, but they may be willing to help you go and grow.

Oftentimes we are given similar visions in order to partner and collaborate with others to make them come to fruition. Seek out those who are either already doing what you desire to do or who share your dream. You can make it happen by partnering together.

Have mentors at each stage or leg of your journey. You may find that you need several different ones but please tap into the wisdom of those that have actually gone before you and done what you desire to do.

Synergy means that the sum of us can accomplish much more than any of us alone. The Bible states that we are one body with many members, and each member is vitally important to the building of the kingdom.

(paraphrased) That passage referred to the church; however, it can be applied to life as well.

Partnering should take place within our homes, on our jobs, in our church and in other walks of life. We definitely need each other to survive.

I've talked about partnering, but what exactly is a partnership? A partnership is an agreement between two or more individuals who will help *each other* to go to the next level or possibly all the way; a marriage, if you will, between two or more people.

A partnership should be based on proven commitments between people.

A partnership in the real sense should not be a one-sided venture. Look for people who not only **say** they are interested in becoming a partner but also **show** their interest. Never partner with anyone who expects you to do all of the giving. That's not a partnership.
We all know that actions speak louder than words.

Referring back to the first chapter, **pray** about the people you have chosen as partners. Ask God if this relationship is one that He is establishing for HIS glory. After receiving your answer proceed into the agreement.

Creflo Dollar states, call no one a friend (partner) unless there is a proven commitment. Know that once you've achieved your goals in pursuit of your purpose many people will want to come on board. Partners are there at the beginning saying, "I believe in you and you believe in me. Together we are going to make some things happen *all* for God's glory." The Bible stresses that whatever we do, we are to do it as unto the Lord. Partnering is a means of doing just that.

In a partnership, it is established that I have your back and you have mine. This can relate to a single project or a lifetime ministry. Each person should bring something to the table. Look for people who are committed.

I've said many times that whenever partnerships take place there should be a roundtable discussion addressing the issues or needs as well as possible solutions. Partnerships can be gifts that keep on giving. What do I mean by that? In a successful partnership, the needs soon diminish as each person looks at what he or she can contribute. Once a meeting or discussion is over each person can walk away with a sense of accomplishment; action items and a knowing that each person is moving forward in joined pursuit of their God-given assignment or purpose.

Partner with businesses that operate in a business manner. I have been so blessed to have partnered with the likes of Black Christian Book Distributors, Kings Highway Web Design, Christian African American Booksellers Association, Affordable Publishing, Women of Purpose and Determination, and Women On the Grow, just to name a few. And as a result of this, I have been able to go and grow.

If your goal or passion is helping others, I encourage you to partner with ministries that share your passion. I've mentioned Jewel Diamond Taylor several times in my writings. I can't begin to thank God for placing her in my life. Because of her influence and messages of hope and encouragement, I continually dare to stretch. The same goes for Annette Jones Davidson (Founder & Director of Women of Purpose and Determination), Felonesecia West (D.I.),

Jackie Graham Chapman, Rose Thornton Kinsey and the entire Women of Purpose and Determination Group.

Partnerships were also established with Pastor W Terrell Snead, II former pastor of The Word of God Baptist Church in Los Angeles and Pastor Ron Hill, pastor of Love and Unity COGIC in Compton. They each have also proven themselves to be ambassadors for kingdom building as well as ones who either has or currently is helping my family and me to grow, grow, and grow.

Those are several examples to show you that by having solid partnerships in place your purpose is not a possibility but a reality. There is no way I could do what I do without the partnerships in my life. There are so many others that I didn't mention. The list is endless.

Look for people who you believe are divine connections from God. Partner with those people and watch what happens. No man is an island.

To close this section, I will share something that was relayed to me recently by a co-worker and fellow church member,

Percy Partee. Prior to my joining Love and Unity, I attended for several months. The services were awesome and I was fed so much spiritually. Well, Percy said that I, along with another mutual friend, was shacking. I thought, "What does he mean?" He readily explained it. When one is shacking they are reaping the benefits of a relationship without the commitment or marriage taking place.
Don't shack, form the partnership.

    Partnership is the fourth key ingredient for pursuing your purpose with passion.

Persist

" . . . the race is not to the swift, nor the battle to the strong, neither yet bread to the wise, nor yet riches to men of understanding, nor yet favour to men of skill: but time and chance happeneth to them all."
Ecclesiastes 9:11

STEP FIVE
Persist

Persistence, persistence, persistence! Persist daily at taking steps towards your journey. Persist when things are going right. Persist when things are going wrong. Be persistent in your journey.

What does it mean to persist? Merriam-Webster's Dictionary states to persist is to go on stubbornly in spite of opposition, importunity, or warning. It further states to persist is to continue to exist especially past a usual, expected or normal time.

Being persistent requires total commitment to your goals or vision. As stated before, even with the best laid plans things don't quite happen some times as we think they should.

Persistence means even though you are not seeing the full manifestation you continue to take steps. Remember inch your way through.

There's another "p" that sometimes wants to stop us dead in our tracks. That "p" is procrastination. Making a decision daily to take some step towards your purpose will eliminate the thought of procrastinating. This is where commitment comes into play; committed to your purpose.

Commitment says I will do it today and will not wait, as by waiting tomorrow may be too late. Procrastination causes us many times to miss opportunities or deadlines. So even if it's uncomfortable or things aren't exactly where you want them to be, persist and commit to the daily steps.

Persist in getting that degree. Your purpose may be becoming an educator. Persist in buying your first home. Your purpose may be becoming a realtor.

Persist in getting that promotion. Your purpose may be one of managing the company. Persist in losing 20 lbs. Your purpose may be becoming a health/fitness expert. Persist in starting your own business. Your purpose may be one of hiring many.

Persist in breaking habits that are detrimental to your health. Persist in taking trips. Persist in becoming financially free. Persist in becoming the biggest giver in your church. Persist in buying that new car.

Persist in buying a home or a car for another family that cannot afford to do it themselves. Your purpose may be to become a philanthropist. Be persistent as in doing so you not only bless yourself and pursue your purpose but you bless others along the way.

Be persistent in education. Strive for doing things in a spirit of excellence. Remember the saying, "If at first you don't succeed try again". Persistence means I'm willing to keep trying.

In "To God Be the Glory" I mentioned the fact that I had a sign that read…"You Never Fail Until You Stop Trying". Persistence means, I will not stop until I reach my goal. Don't stop. Keep moving.

A few weeks ago, Terry McNulty (another co-worker and church member) and I started walking during lunch. I had not walked or done any exercise in several months. Determined that I was/am going to lose weight and get fit, we headed out. During the second week we had gone to the park and I just could not make that full lap around the park. I applauded myself for going half-way BUT Terry said something so simple yet so profound. She said to me that I had to press beyond the pain or press in spite of the pain. These may not be her exact words but the gist of it is when you are persistently pursuing your purpose, there will be many times you will have to press beyond the pain. Persistence pays off.

Promote

To advance in station, rank, or honor:
To contribute to the growth or
prosperity of:
To help bring into being
Merriam-Webster's Online Dictionary

STEP SIX
Promote

Be the biggest advocate or promoter in pursuing your purpose. Sometimes this may mean you are the ONLY promoter. That, my friend, is okay because this is about YOU pursuing YOUR purpose with passion.

Say it. Speak it. Tell it to those who have similar visions and dreams and to those who can help to make it become a reality. Avoid those who try to pull you down or don't fully support you. Some refer to them as haters. I say they are people who cannot see what you see.

Do not believe the lies of the enemy. When he whispers all of the reasons you can't pursue your purpose, respond back with a sound, "Yes, I can!" The enemy often disguises himself as well meaning people. Don't listen to what they say. You've prayed. You've prepared. You've planned and prioritized. You've established sound partnerships. Now it's time to promote yourself as if your life depended on it. Reality check - it really does.

The Bible tells us that God is no respecter of person. If any one person has ever accomplished what you are pursuing, so can you. Surround yourself with people who encourage you. Remember in Genesis, God *said* and then He *saw*. Promotion is saying it over and over again. Soon you'll see it.

Those of us who have the God kind of faith can call those things that be not as though they were. There is power in the tongue. So promote yourself, your vision, and your dream.

Bible scholars know the story of Joseph. Joseph was a dreamer who shared his dream with his brothers. He never imagined what would happen to him. He was sold into slavery, falsely accused and imprisoned all because he chose to tell his dream. But it didn't end there. Because God had given the dream to him, he faithfully brought it to pass at the appointed time. Don't only dream but speak it. Just be sure you have followed the other steps first. That way you are assured that you are speaking it to the right people.

Be enthusiastic about your endeavor. Surround yourself with the real "movers and shakers". We all know some. They're just "can-do" people. You know those that SAY I can do all things through Christ who gives me strength and while SAYING or PROMOTING themselves they are actually walking the walk.

Let's look at some people we can all relate to who have dared to promote themselves while pursuing their purpose and have "arrived": Tyler Perry, Steve Harvey, Joyce Meyer, Fantasia Barrino, Oprah Winfrey, Sam Walton, Tyra Banks, Bishop T D Jakes, Jewel Diamond Taylor, President Barack Obama, and so many more. They all faced and conquered obstacles as well as endured hardships to see their dreams manifest.

My point to you is this - no one is going to promote YOU like YOU can promote yourself. The people listed above have defied all odds and walked through the exact or similar steps I'm giving you.

You should be roused from your sleep with questions as to what is your purpose and what are you doing to pursue it coming at you and immediately spout the answer. No one knows your purpose better than you.

Promote yourself, your business, your ministry, your purpose. PROMOTE YOU!

Patience

"Wherefore seeing we also are compassed about with so great a cloud of witnesses, let us lay aside every weight, and the sin which doth so easily beset us, and let us run with *patience* the race that is set before us. Looking unto Jesus the author and finisher of our faith . . . "
Hebrews 12:1,2

STEP SEVEN
Patience

Oh my God, now she's saying to be patient! After doing all of these things there may be times you'll have to wait? Galatians 5 tells us that patience is one of the fruit of the Spirit. In Luke 8:15 Jesus speaks these words, "But that on the good ground are they, which in an honest and good heart, having heard the word, keep it and bring forth fruit with **patience**."

Let's focus on the latter scripture. Jesus is saying that we are on good ground when we are honest, have a good heart, hear the word (praying/preparing), and keep it (planning/prioritizing/persisting/promoting and partnering). He goes on to say that we will bring forth fruit with patience. What is fruit? It's the manifestation of a thing.

Fruit can be different things to different people, depending on the purpose. One thing both scriptures let us know that there are times when we will have to wait patiently for the manifestations. Joseph waited. Job waited. Esther waited. There will be many times when we will need patience in our lives.

Remember, we are not waiting on man. We're waiting on God. At that set time the vision will speak. It will not lie. We have to do our part and trust God to do His part in His own time and in his own way.

I love the illustration that Bishop T D Jakes used in one of his sermons. He said when we are waiting on God for the manifestation we should not be tapping our watches and saying to ourselves, "God, you know I'm waiting." He continued to say that we should be waiting as a servant, referring to a waiter carrying a tray.

We must have patience in pursuing our purpose. The race is not given to the swift. We have to be willing to endure, with patience, the race that is set before us as we look unto Jesus as the author and finisher of our faith.

So far we've covered prayer, preparation, planning/prioritizing, partnerships, persistence, promoting, and patience. We are all well on our way now in pursuit of our purposes.

Remember when you're trying to rush some things to make them happen, **patience** is necessary in pursuing your purpose with passion.

Promises

"For God is not unrighteous to forget your work and labor of love, which ye have shown toward his name, in that ye have ministered to the saints, and do minister. And we desire that every one of you do show the same diligence to the full assurance of hope unto the end. That ye be not slothful, but followers of them who through faith and patience inherit the promises."
Hebrews 6:10-12

"For ye had need of patience, that, after ye have done the will of God, ye might receive the promise.
Hebrews 10:36

STEP EIGHT
Promises

Hurray! We've finally gotten here. This is the step we are all aiming for. After following the seven steps listed you will receive the promises. I keep reminding you the word in Habakkuk states the vision will speak, it will not lie.

Read the promises of God in the Word for yourself. Claim the promises of God in the Word for yourself. Repeat the promises of God daily to yourself. Follow the steps outlined in this booklet and you WILL fulfill your divine calling and pursue **YOUR** purpose with passion as never before.

Step outside the box. God declares the end at the beginning.

Become a philanthropist while attaining the promises. Look for ways to help others who are less fortunate. Remember, God blesses us to be a blessing.

Find a worthwhile cause to support. Support your local church and local charities. As God provides the increase, enlarge your territory and support ministries that are doing worldwide activities. Our ultimate purpose in life is found in Matthew 18:20 which tells us to go into all the world reaching, teaching and assisting others while telling them about God and His goodness. You may not be physically able to go yourself; however, by supporting ministries that are, you are still fulfilling the great commission.

Now that you have these tips, get fired up and determined to fulfill your God-given, God-inspired, God-driven purpose with passion like never before. Come on! You can do it! I believe in you!

Our ultimate "pay-off" will be when each of us meets the Master face to face and hear Him say, "Well done, thy good and faithful one. You have finally finished the race."

Pastor W. Terrell Snead, II says:
Pursue your purpose with—

<u>Prayer</u> knowing it is God who will give you the <u>Power</u> you need.

<u>Patience</u>, knowing it is God who will give you the <u>Peace</u> you need.

<u>Passion,</u> knowing it is God who will make the <u>Provisions</u> you need, and

<u>Persistence,</u> knowing it is God who will make you <u>Prominent</u> among great people.

Now that you've read the book begin to SOAR—**S**ee **O**ver- **A**verage **R**esults take place in your life. And as you SOAR, remember to always **<u>Praise GOD!</u>**

Conclusion

You are now ready to give birth to the dreams and visions God has placed inside of you. If you are a woman who's ever given birth to a child, you too will go through a similar range of emotions in pursuing your purpose.

The first stage will be excitement or possibly denial depending on the situation. The second stage will be acceptance and the beginning preparations for your new arrival.

You will make doctor's visits, eat healthier, exercise, and do all of the things to prepare for your baby.

The closer it gets to the delivery date, the harder it gets. These are the times when the mumbling (I can't wait to have this baby); the grumbling (When will this child get here); and the complaining (I'll never do this again).
The pain intensifies and you're just ready for the baby to come.

Guess what though? Once you've actually given birth, after the many declarations that you will never have another child again, you look at that bundle of joy and all of the pain is soon forgotten. And you find yourself pregnant again later.

The same is true as you stretch in your journey; you will go through a range of emotions and you may declare to any and every one that you'll never stretch again. But once the manifestation of one thing takes place and as you celebrate the accomplishment/birth, you soon find yourself pregnant again. The pain from giving birth the first time is soon forgotten.

And you pray, prepare, plan, prioritize, partner, have patience and continue the process basically all over again. And you SOAR higher and higher! Keep SOAR'ing!

I leave you with this shared by Annette Jones-Davidson; as you pursue your purpose with passion think of traveling. If you leave South Carolina traveling to Louisiana as she has numerous times, don't be in a hurry to get there. Stop a few times and enjoy the trip even when you have to arrive there by a certain date and time.

At one point, when she first started traveling, her mind was so set on getting to her destination that she hurriedly got from point A to point B; sometimes driving straight through without ever stopping. As she's gotten older, she now still has her eyes focused on her destination BUT she's learned to leave a bit earlier, stop along the way, sometimes for a meal or to shop or just to see a new place she's never seen before, still arriving at the set time. Enjoy your journey.

Regina G. Mixon

Suggested Readings

1. Covey, S. (1980). The 7 Habits of Highly Effective People. New York. Fireside
2. Warren, R. (2002). The Purpose Driven Life. Grand Rapids. Zondervan
3. Osteen, J. (2004). Your Best Life Now. New York. Warner Faith
4. Jakes, T. (2007). Reposition Yourself. New York. Atria Books
5. Taylor, J. (1998). Sisterfriends. East St. Louis. Quiet Time
6. Meyer, J. (2005). Approval Addiction. New York. Warner Faith
7. Mixon, R. (2007). To God Be the Glory. San Diego. Affordable

www.ingramcontent.com/pod-product-compliance
Lightning Source LLC
Chambersburg PA
CBHW032018290426
44109CB00013B/709